Kos - A Gem in the Aegean Sea

Stig Ulrichsen

Published by Nunatak, 2024.

KOS - A GEM IN THE AEGEAN SEA

First edition. December 1, 2024.

Copyright © 2024 Stig Ulrichsen.

ISBN: 978-8792840271

Written by Stig Ulrichsen.

Table of Contents

To my beloved family.

Kos - A Gem in the Aegean Sea

TRAVEL ADVENTURES, Hidden Tips, and Historical Insights!

Cover Photo: Anna Klápštová

Welcome to Kos, the Aegean jewel where history is as colorful as a rainbow and the island's heartbeat thumps with the energy of a lively Zorba dance. Nestled southeast of the Greek mainland, framed by the Dodecanese Islands, and embraced by crystal-clear waters, Kos invites you to swim with dolphins and waltz with mermaids. This is the island where stepping ashore feels like entering a grand theatrical production—nature as the set designer, and history as the star performer.

The rugged mountain ridge, more dramatic than a Greek tragedy, was separated from its kin during a volcanic extravaganza where the earth's crust pirouetted like a Greek god performing ballet. Explore rock formations and ancient geological layers, where fossils of bygone mammals rest like slumbering Olympians. Kos is not just a landscape; it's a living stage, especially at Kamara Bay, where even the rhythm of earthquakes seems to make seasoned dancers quake in their sandals.

The island unfurls like a catwalk, with Mount Dikeo as its proud supermodel. Peaks like Vourkna, Kefála, Skenteri, Mavrovouni, and Latra call out to adventurous souls, daring them to embark on a haute couture expedition. Meanwhile, the ruins of the Knights of St. John castle at Thimiana stand like vintage fashion pieces, timeless and elegant in their own way.

The coastline, kissed by the Carpathian Sea, resembles an impressionist masterpiece with strokes of Cape Psalidi, Cape Skandário, Aghios Fokas, and Aghios Stefanos, all choreographed into a natural ballet.

1

Agriculture, livestock, fishing, and tourism combine to form a gastronomic menu where Kos serves up succulent vegetables, golden vineyards, olive groves, and orchards as the main course. Fishermen's craft adds a symphony of seafood delights straight from the ocean depths.

The fishing trade beats strong on Kos, exporting fresh catches to bustling fish markets in Piraeus and Thessaloniki. Amidst this picturesque harmony lies the largest fishing hub in the Dodecanese and one of the Mediterranean's top salt-extraction centers—where even the sea salt adds a flavorful note to Kos' culinary opus.

So, dive into this dance with history, swim alongside mermaids, and let the flavors of Kos' bounty enchant your taste buds. Here, you're not just a tourist; you're the leading role in the island's eternal waltz, where every moment is an adventure, and the past and present move in perfect harmony like the most graceful of Greek gods.

My Personal Adventure on Kos

—

MY JOURNEY TO KOS BEGAN when my trusty companion René and I decided to hop aboard the adventure plane bound for the island in mid-September 1989. Yes, I know—it's been so long that even the pyramids would gasp, "Whoa, that's old school!" But trust me, we were more excited than a cat on a diving board, ready to leap into the vibrant 90s Greece with all the glitz and giggles we could muster. Our goals were as simple as a sunset gyro: savor great food, meet wonderful people (hopefully with plenty of sunscreen), relax by the massive blue swimming pool with its refreshing water and breathtaking sea views, and explore Kos Town and its charming mountain villages.

Speaking of exploration, here's a little story. At our hotel, we met some fantastic people, including Henrik, who wanted to join us on an adventure while his wife stayed behind to soak up the sun. The three of us hatched a plan for a moped expedition that would make us feel like modern-day Greek heroes—or maybe more like Don Quixote on two wheels.

The next day, under a sun so hot it could grill more than just a souvlaki, we rented three mopeds and hit the winding roads toward Asklepion. This fascinating archaeological treasure rests on a secluded hilltop, surrounded by majestic cypress trees and an air of endless tranquility. It's one of Greece's most significant ruins, rivaling even Athens' Acropolis.

Unfortunately, the sanctuary was about as open as a Greek budget meeting on a Monday. After admiring its beauty from a distance through the locked iron gates, we hopped back on our mopeds. Soon, the engines purred like Greek bouzoukis as we powered up the steep roads to a deserted mountain village. The streets were emptier than a barrel of feta after a Greek wedding, with only the shadows of locals lounging in the heat.

Suddenly, we spotted an elderly woman waving us over with a smile as warm as the Aegean sun. She welcomed us into her home, which doubled as a quaint little restaurant. Here, canned beer reigned as king, and a massive pot of tomato soup held court as queen. Dusting ourselves off, we washed our hands as she ladled out the soup with a touch of magic. To this day, it remains the best tomato soup I've ever tasted—a soup so divine even Zeus himself would trade a lightning bolt for a spoonful.

We soaked up the silence and reveled in the thought of having discovered a place more authentic than a Greek tragedy. But just as we left cash on the table to pay for this magical experience and headed back to our mopeds, parked on the roadside, reality struck us like a flying feta ball.

Tour buses, packed with tourists who looked like a flock of hungry seagulls, had descended on the village. The authenticity evaporated faster than Greek yogurt in the midday sun.

"So much for our Robinson Crusoe moment," we thought, laughing as we zoomed back to our base, Hotel Okeanis—now rebranded as TUI BLUE Oceanis Beach.

That trip sparked my lifelong love affair with Kos and Greece. I've visited so many times since that I feel almost more Greek than Zeus himself. You know what I mean, right? In 1991, I published a travel guide titled *Ultima Rejseguide: Kos*, a black-and-white relic of its time. Printing in color was a luxury back then, but now, I aim to bring some vibrancy and humor to those words—like a Greek dance on a sunlit day.

Here's my updated travel guide, filled with my best tips, so you can use it to plan your own adventure. Hop on and let the journey begin. Bon voyage! Or as they say in Greek, καλό ταξίδι!

– Stig Ulrichsen, January 2024

Kos – A Quick Overview

KOS STANDS PROUDLY northwest of the awe-inspiring island of Rhodes, just 10 kilometers from the historic coast of Turkey. Covering an area of 295 km², this dolphin-shaped island serves as a playground for approximately 30,000 residents.

Kos International Airport "Hippocrates"

Nestled near Antimachia, about 27 kilometers from the historic Kos Town, the island's airport bears the name of the legendary physician Hippocrates. It first opened its doors on April 4, 1964, with a modest 1,200-meter runway. Its mission was simple: connect the island to the world and fuel the booming tourism industry.

In 1973, the runway was extended to 2,390 meters, welcoming larger passenger planes and even greater adventures. By 1980, a new terminal emerged as part of the modernization efforts—an architectural landmark that mirrors the character of Kos itself. Summers now bring a flurry of charter flights, with approximately two million eager tourists arriving annually to bask in the island's sun-drenched beaches, explore its cultural treasures, and soak up its unique charm.

The Verdant Landscape and Rich History of Kos

Kos offers a mild, lush landscape where nature and human hands have collaborated beautifully. Here, orchards, vegetable fields, and farmlands shift with the seasons, creating a tapestry of vibrant colors. While the dramatic cliffs of other Greek islands are absent, Kos' plains and rolling hills have their own quiet allure.

The mountains, crowned by Mount Dikaios Hristos, beckon hikers with promises of thrilling adventures. Other peaks like Skenten, Kefala, Mavrovouni, and Latra are also waiting to be explored. The island's flora, particularly the aromatic herbs once used by Hippocrates in his treatments, captivate nature enthusiasts.

Stretching along its 110-kilometer coastline, Kos boasts a variety of idyllic beaches such as Tigaki, Magic Beach, Paradise Beach, Kardamena, and Mastichari. Each beach tells its own story, from Tigaki's crashing waves to the tranquil, family-friendly waters of Kardamena.

Kos Town and Its Cultural Gems

A stroll through Kos Town unveils layer upon layer of history. Rebuilt in 1934 after a devastating earthquake, the town now offers a delightful blend of ancient ruins, Roman villas, bathhouses, and temples. Along the palm-lined promenades by the harbor, you'll find charming tavernas, bouzouki bars, and inviting restaurants.

Casa Romana, a beautifully restored villa, showcases stunning mosaics depicting marine life. Meanwhile, the **Castle of the Knights of St. John**, built in 1391, stands as a sentinel over the town, reminding visitors of bygone threats. The Turkish mosque district offers a glimpse into daily life and devotion, while the square featuring Hippocrates' statue and an intricate mosaic is worth a stop.

The market is another highlight—a covered oasis bursting with Mediterranean fruits, vegetables, and butcher stalls, all infused with an atmosphere you won't want to miss.

Discovering Kos by Bike

KOS IS CELEBRATED AS a cyclist-friendly island, making it easy to rent a bike and pedal through its stunning landscapes. One highlight is **Kefalos**, where an old windmill offers panoramic views that will leave you breathless. Another must-see is **Agios Stefanos**, home to the island's most picturesque bay. For something unique, head to **Agios Fokas**, where black-sand beaches provide a striking contrast to the sparkling blue waters and offer spectacular views of nearby islands and the Turkish coastline.

The economy of Kos is rooted in tourism, agriculture, and fishing. The island produces abundant quantities of wine, grapes, honey, and vegetables, delighting both locals and their neighbors with its bountiful harvests.

The Magical World of Mythology on Kos

DIVE INTO THE ENCHANTING world of mythology on Kos, where giants and demigods intertwine, and the island's history blends seamlessly with tales of heaven and earth. In ancient Greek religion, giants were not just mythical creatures but the offspring of Uranus (the Sky) and Gaia (the Earth). An epic battle—**the Gigantomachy**—pitted these formidable beings against the mighty Olympian gods, ending in the giants' defeat and relentless pursuit.

One such giant, **Polyvotis**, sought refuge on Kos after his loss. However, Poseidon, the god of the sea, chased him in a fit of fury. Tearing a piece of Kos from the earth, Poseidon hurled it at the fleeing giant, creating **Nisyros**, a volcanic island northwest of Kos. This blend of myth and geology offers a breathtaking tale where legend and reality converge.

Other giants, known as the **Titans**, also found sanctuary on Kos after their struggle against the Olympians. Among them were **Kynnos**, **Phebus**, and **Korios**, whose presence lent the island its mythological name, **Kynnis**. Kos became a pivotal location in Greek mythology, particularly tied to the demigod **Heracles**, son of Zeus and Alcmene.

Heracles, renowned for his extraordinary feats and all-too-human flaws, came to Kos after a tragic episode where, in a fit of madness, he killed his own children. Seeking redemption, he arrived on the island, only to clash with a young shepherd named **Antagoras**. Their conflict escalated into a battle involving Heracles' companions and the island's inhabitants. After the chaos, Heracles sought refuge in a remote village, disguised as a woman to evade his enemies.

The **city-state of Fixioi** provided a sanctuary for Heracles, and through a mix of hospitality and cunning, he emerged as a king. His bravery and determination left an indelible mark on Kos, weaving his name and deeds into the island's rich history. The legacy of Heracles continued through his descendants, including his son **Thessalos**, who later ruled over both Kos and Nisyros.

The History of Kos

KOS IN THE EMBRACE of Pelasgian Prehistory

Step into the prehistoric shadows of Kos, where the island's early days are veiled in the mists of time, and the mysteries of the Stone Age have been lost to the ages. Much of Kos' prehistory remains an enigma, as earthquakes and the ravages of time have erased many traces of its ancient past. To glimpse the earliest days of Kos, we rely on mythology and the poetic accounts of ancient writers.

The **Carians**, one of the oldest Greek tribes, are believed to have been the island's first inhabitants. Kos' original name, **Kouris** or **Karis**, reflects their presence. The **Pelasgians**, a proud people from Thessaly and among the first Greek settlers, also left their mark on Kos. Ruins at **Paleoskala** and **Agios Fokas** bear witness to their culture and early influence on the island.

Triopas I, described as wise and intelligent, became the first king of Kos, leading the Pelasgians on their journey from Thessaly and laying the foundation for a legacy that later rulers would build upon. During the reign of **Triopas II**, the island flourished in a golden age, forming alliances, including one with Minoan Crete, which solidified Kos' position in the region.

The arrival of the **Achaeans**, an Indo-European people, brought significant change to Kos. After conquering Crete, the Achaeans extended their dominance to the Aegean islands, including Kos, marking a new era of influence on the island's society.

One notable king of Kos, **Eurypylos II**, is remembered both in mythology and in Homer's epics. His reign and his death in battle with

Heracles shaped the destiny of Kos. Heracles' marriage to **Chalciope** introduced a new ruling lineage—the **Asclepiadae**.

Following the Trojan War, **Podalirius**, son of the legendary healer **Asclepius**, sought refuge on Kos after surviving a shipwreck. He founded the Asclepiadae dynasty, and its 18th descendant was the famous **Hippocrates**, who later established Kos as a center of medical knowledge.

Doric Dominance on Kos

In the 12th century BCE, the **Dorians**, the third wave of Greek settlers, arrived, displacing the Achaeans and establishing their presence in much of the Aegean. The Dorians settled on islands such as Aegina, Kythera, Milos, Thera (Santorini), Crete, Rhodes, and Kos. The historian **Strabo** confirms the dominance of Doric language and culture on these islands, including Kos, which embraced this new cultural direction.

Kos experienced economic and cultural growth during this period, aided by its fertile soil and the influence of diverse cultures. Strabo describes Kos as an island where agriculture, livestock farming, fishing, and even silk production thrived. Several important cities, such as **Pamphylis**, **Antimacheia**, and **Esthmioton**, emerged, with their inhabitants devoted to worshiping deities like **Demeter** and **Asclepius**, the god of medicine and healing.

In the 7th century BCE, the Dorians established the **Hexapolis**, or "League of Six Cities," which included Kos, Knidos, Halicarnassus, Ialysos, Kamiros, Lindos, Kalymnos, and Nisyros. This alliance served both economic and religious purposes, with its religious center located at the **Temple of Apollo** near Cape Triopion.

Kos expanded its influence by founding colonies in southern Italy, notably in **Daunia**. The independent spirit and wisdom of the Kosians were demonstrated when they refused to hand over a precious golden tripod they had captured, instead presenting it to the philosopher **Thales**. This act became a symbol of Kos' autonomy and intelligence.

In the 6th century BCE, Kos underwent political changes and embraced democracy, influenced by the Athenian laws of **Solon**. Although the **Persian Empire** gained control over parts of Greece in the 5th century BCE, Kos refused to support the Persian wars against Greece, earning enmity from the Persians.

The Doric period of Kos' history was marked by cultural and political prosperity, establishing the island as a significant hub in the Aegean Sea.

From Heroic Spirits to Cultural Transformation

KOS AND QUEEN ARTEMISIA'S Persian Alliance

In a distant past, when legends enveloped islands like cosmic pearls, the destiny of Kos became intertwined with **Queen Artemisia of Caria**, an ally of the Persian King Darius. Following an Apollonian thread of fate, Kos was drawn into the heart of the Persian war machine. Five ships from the island joined **Xerxes' fleet**, which sought to crush Greece. In 480 BCE, Kos bore witness to the decisive **Battle of Salamis**, where Greek forces triumphed over the Persians. A year later, in 479 BCE, the **Battle of Mycale** saw the Persians decisively defeated, liberating several islands and securing Kos' place in Greece's victory.

In 477 BCE, Kos became part of the **Delian League**, an alliance led by Athens. From 468 BCE, the island entered a period of growth and prosperity. Proud and fiercely independent, the Kosians refused to aid the Persians during a devastating epidemic, demonstrating their loyalty to Greece and their commitment to freedom.

During the **Peloponnesian War** (431–404 BCE), Kos allied with Athens, symbolically contributing an annual tribute of five talents. However, in 411 BCE, the Spartan fleet under **Astyochus** invaded the island, plunging it into turmoil. Many inhabitants fled to **Astypalaia**, and soon after, a devastating earthquake struck the island. Athens responded with aid, sending supplies and funds under **Alcibiades** to rebuild Kos. A defensive wall was constructed around the city, but many residents relocated from the old center, heeding the advice of the great physician **Hippocrates** to settle in safer areas.

Kos' Mycenaean past left its mark on the landscape, with golden fragments from geometric tombs serving as reminders of its rich history. **Aristotle** described Kos as a bustling hub, while **Strabo** praised it as the best-constructed city among the Aegean islands.

In 405 BCE, **Lysander's victory** brought Kos under Spartan control, but in 394 BCE, Admiral **Conon**'s triumph at the **Battle of Knidos** spurred a new economic revival for the island. Kos became a center for learning and culture, where music, gymnastics, and athleticism shaped young minds, and prizes from athletic competitions elevated many to hero status.

Kos' Intellectual and Artistic Zenith

This period saw the rise of many renowned figures from Kos, including **Epicharmus**, the founder of Sicilian comedy, and **Irontas**, a poet known for his depictions of society's lower classes. Most famously, **Hippocrates**, the father of medicine, put Kos on the global map with his groundbreaking theories and practices. The artist **Apelles**, celebrated for his painting of **Aphrodite Rising from the Sea**, further cemented Kos' place in artistic history.

However, with great achievement often comes envy. In 358 BCE, **Mausolus of Halicarnassus** arrived with his troops and, in secret collaboration with local oligarchs, abolished democracy on Kos. He established a military autocracy, leading to the closure of schools and the decline of a once-vibrant cultural era.

Alexander the Great's Allure Over Kos

In 334 BCE, Kos became part of the stormy era of **Alexander the Great**, forging close ties with the Macedonian empire. Despite the alliance, the island's assembly continued to appoint its own governors, ensuring autonomy and security.

In 333 BCE, **Persian forces** briefly captured Kos under the command of the Rhodian general **Memnon**, but freedom was swiftly restored by Alexander's troops, led by **Ptolemy**. A year later, in 332 BCE, the Persians attempted another conquest, but Alexander's navy secured a decisive victory, stabilizing Kos' future within the Greek kingdom.

Legend has it that the Kosian physician **Critodemos** saved Alexander from death in India, earning the island a place in the conqueror's heart. Kos minted coins bearing Alexander's image as a tribute, further cementing its ties to his legacy. Other medical luminaries from Kos, such as **Erasistratos**, **Nicas**, and **Dexippos**, continued the island's tradition of advancing medicine.

The poet **Theocritus**, a descendant of the Kosian physician Simos, also left his mark during this era. Born in Sicily in 310 BCE, Theocritus' pastoral verses vividly captured the joys and sorrows of rural life, immortalizing the island's spirit in poetry.

After Alexander's death, Kos fell under the rule of **Antigonus** but continued to thrive. Laws were refined, making the island a model of social order and prosperity. In 311 BCE, Kos formed an alliance with **Egypt**, under **Ptolemy**, forcing Antigonus to relinquish control.

In 309 BCE, Ptolemy and his family wintered on Kos, where Queen **Berenice** gave birth to **Ptolemy II**, a future king of Egypt. In 306 BCE, Ptolemy's forces defeated **Demetrius Poliorcetes**, bringing Kos back into the Egyptian kingdom.

Kos' Resilience Amidst Conflict

The 3rd century BCE brought new challenges. In 266 BCE, **Antigonus Gonatas** seized Kos, and in 220 BCE, the island participated in the **First Macedonian War** against **Philip V**. Kos joined forces with Rhodes, Kalymnos, and Nisyros, forging a regional alliance.

By 205–204 BCE, Kos, Kalymnos, and Nisyros formed a harmonious union, with Kos as the leading center. In 197 BCE, Kos and Rhodes allied with **Rome** against Philip V, and during the **Third Macedonian War** (171 BCE), Kos joined forces with Rhodes and Rome once again.

Despite the tumult of war, Kos flourished. In 122 BCE, **Cleopatra**, Queen of Egypt, visited the island and entrusted her treasures to the **Asclepeion**, Kos' famed sanctuary of medicine.

This peaceful era ended abruptly in 88 BCE, when **Mithridates of Pontus** attacked Kos with brutal force. He plundered the city, seized Cleopatra's treasures, and set the Asclepeion ablaze. Yet Kos continued its journey through history, now under the influence of the Roman Empire, which would shape the next chapter of the island's story.

A Part of the Roman Empire

DURING THE CAPTIVATING era of the mighty **Roman Empire**, Kos emerged as a unique province with distinctive rights and influence. The island gained prominence, especially after **Emperor Antony**, charmed by its allure, recognized its inhabitants as proud Roman citizens, granting them full privileges. This elevated Kos to a meeting place for some of the most influential figures of the time.

In **38 BCE**, **Herod the Great**, the Jewish tetrarch, visited Kos, marking the beginning of a flourishing period under his protection. Later, the citizens secured favor with **Emperor Tiberius** by supporting him in his conflict with the Senate. In **32 BCE**, the **Asclepeion** was officially recognized as a sanctuary, and in gratitude, the citizens erected an impressive monument honoring Herod, inscribed with their thanks.

Under **Emperor Augustus** in **30 BCE**, Kos experienced a shift. Its inhabitants were required to revere the emperor and his daughter, Julia, as the goddess Artemis. Although Kos continued to enjoy special privileges, its people had to adapt to the shifting political landscape of the Roman Empire.

During **Nero's reign**, a temple was erected in his honor on Kos, and the people were compelled to worship him as a deity. However, after Nero's downfall, this practice was abandoned. The island also faced natural disasters, including a devastating earthquake in **27 BCE** that destroyed large parts of Kos and deepened the general decline of the period.

Despite these challenges, Kos continued to serve the Roman Empire faithfully, earning tax exemptions and other rewards. The physician **Xenophon** healed **Emperor Claudius**, and in return, Kos was granted exemption from taxes. As part of the agreement, the island sent artworks to Rome, including **Apelles'** famous painting *The Birth of Aphrodite*, which was revered in the emperor's temple, according to the historian **Strabo**.

Between **69–79 CE**, under **Emperor Vespasian, Rhodes** was designated as the metropolis of the Aegean, and Kos was governed by Roman administrators. Despite this, Kos maintained its cultural pride and economic vitality, with agriculture, livestock farming, craftsmanship, and trade thriving.

During the reign of **Diocletian** (284–305 CE), known for his persecution of Christians, the emperor proclaimed himself "Augustus" to strengthen the empire. He divided power among four co-emperors to improve administration. Despite the Christian persecution, uncertainty and violence led to a growing number of converts, with Kos' inhabitants actively participating in the Christian movement.

When Diocletian retired in **305 CE**, civil wars erupted within the Roman Empire. **Constantine**, ruling the western part of the empire alongside **Maxentius**, defeated Maxentius in **312 CE** and embraced Christianity after his victory. As emperor, Constantine issued laws granting Christians the right to practice their religion freely, culminating in the **Edict of Milan** in **313 CE**, which legalized Christianity across the empire.

Christianity began to take root on Kos, with legends claiming that **Saint Paul** visited the island during his travels, preaching the gospel under the famous **plane tree of Hippocrates**. Stories also tell of **Saint Xenia**, who fled to Kos to escape her wealthy father's wrath before continuing to Asia Minor, where she found refuge in a monastery.

Years later, in **1085**, **Saint Christodoulos** founded a monastery in the old village of Pyli on Kos. The island continued to be a vital religious and cultural center for centuries to come.

Byzantine Era and Venetian Rule

———

IN **324 CE**, **Constantine the Great** achieved a decisive victory over **Licinius** after a protracted civil war. This triumph transformed not only Kos but the entire Roman Empire. As emperor, Constantine made a monumental decision: he declared **Christianity** the official religion of the empire and gave the city of Byzantium a new and enchanting name—**Constantinople**. This marked the beginning of the grand **Byzantine Empire**.

Kos, a beautiful gem in the Mediterranean, became a province of this new empire. The Byzantine emperors ushered in an era of peace and prosperity for the island. However, despite this, Kos remained vulnerable to attacks from the enemies of Byzantium. **Slavs**, **Bulgars**, **Saracens**, **Genoese**, **Venetians**, **Crusaders**, **Arabs**, and **Turks** all targeted Kos, battering the island like relentless waves against a fragile boat.

In **554 CE**, a devastating earthquake struck, destroying much of Kos. The Byzantine historian **Agathias** described the island as a landscape of ruins in the aftermath. Kos' cultural flourishing was abruptly interrupted, and like many other Greek cities, it entered a period of decline.

And Then Came the Turks

IN THE KALEIDOSCOPE of history, one of the most turbulent chapters for Kos unfolded under **Turkish rule**, casting long shadows over the island. After the Venetian control ended, a new conqueror arrived—a fateful day, **June 3, 1457**.

Like a violent storm, **18,000 Turkish warriors** landed on the shores of Kos. With **156 ships** loaded with formidable weapons and led by the fearsome Admiral **Hamza**, they targeted the fortresses at **Pyli**, **Kefalos**, and **Antimachia**. Despite the defenders' brave resistance and unyielding determination, their strongholds were plundered, and the inhabitants fled in chaos.

The Turks' hunger for conquest was insatiable. They returned, this time under the command of **Mehmet II**, but once again, Kos refused to submit. The **papal fleet**, led by **Lodovico Scarampi**, liberated several oppressed islands, temporarily freeing Kos. Even the mighty Turks could not match the **Knights of St. John from Malta**, who resisted their attacks.

However, in **December 1522**, after months of relentless siege, the knights of **Lango**—as Kos was also called—finally fell to the Turks. In **1523**, **Sultan Suleiman** renamed the island ”**Stankoöy**“, ushering in a brutal period of dominance. Their violent oppression, however, could not crush the inhabitants' pride. The people of Kos seized every opportunity to remind their oppressors that only Greeks should cultivate the island's land.

Despite tragedies such as the execution of **Johannes Nafkliros**, burned at the stake in **1609**, and the devastating explosion of a dynamite stockpile in **1816**, the people remained steadfast. Schools on Kos reopened and operated until **1821**, a sign of resilience amid oppression.

The people of Kos never lost hope for freedom. Waving Greek flags against the odds, they stood with Greek freedom fighters like **Miaoulis** and **Sahtouris**. At **Cape Skandario**, they defeated the Egyptian fleet led by **Ismail Gibraltar**, though many Kosians paid the ultimate price for liberty.

The yoke of tyranny weighed heavily on Kos, and news of successful uprisings on the mainland incited Turkish rage. Heroic freedom fighters on Kos were brutally executed, many hanged from the iconic **plane tree of Hippocrates**. A special stone, known as **"Kako Prinari"** (*The Evil Oak*), became a lasting symbol of resistance and freedom, bearing the scars of this violent chapter even today.

The Illusion of Italian Liberators

IN THE SPRING OF **1912**, as the sea breeze danced along Kos' shores, the island's destiny took another dramatic turn. **Italian forces** arrived, driving out the Turkish conquerors and offering renewed hope to Kos' people. Welcoming the Italians as liberators, the inhabitants dreamed of uniting with Greece. A resolution was presented, and the Italians seemingly agreed, promising that Kos would remain Greek and that the oppressive Turkish rule would never again cast its shadow over the island.

But this joy was fleeting, like flowers wilting under a scorching sun. When **Mussolini** rose to power in **1918**, the Italian fascists transformed into new tyrants on Kos. The land was confiscated and lay unused, claimed by the Italian state. Economic hardship deepened under heavy taxes, and Greek schools—once filled with the laughter of learning—were closed one by one. Students were forced to join "**Balilla**", the fascist youth organization, to continue their education. Only a few brave souls received secret lessons.

The Italian language infiltrated schools, and the authorities sought to mold Kos' children into loyal followers of the Italian regime. Religious freedom was stifled, and ordaining priests was forbidden, prompting a slow erosion of faith across the island.

In **1934**, a devastating earthquake struck Kos, destroying **80% of the island's houses**. Italian architects were brought in to rebuild the city, and while Kos rose from the ruins, it bore the marks of a new architectural style imposed by its occupiers.

When Mussolini fell, the people of Kos hoped freedom was finally within reach. The island briefly came under **British control**, but only for

23

20 days, before the **Germans** seized Kos on **October 3, 1943**. The next **18 months** were some of the darkest in Kos' history, with famine and fear spreading across the island.

On **May 9, 1945**, Kos was liberated by British forces, and on **March 7, 1948**, the island was finally united with its motherland, Greece—a long-awaited light at the end of a stormy tunnel. The people of Kos could finally breathe freely again, and in **1981**, the island became part of the **European Union**, alongside the rest of Greece.

Key Historical Milestones of Kos

HERE IS A CONCISE OVERVIEW of Kos' remarkable history, presented through key dates that together form a vivid tapestry of the island's rich past:

- **700 BCE**: Kos joins the **Hexapolis**, the League of Six Cities, alongside islands like Halicarnassus. This military and commercial alliance strengthens Kos' influence in the region, leveraging its strategic location to become a dominant force in trade and politics.

- **477 BCE**: Following the **Battle of Salamis**, Kos joins the **Delian League**, led by Athens. This marks a new political era as the island alternates between supporting Athens and Sparta, depending on shifting alliances in the chaotic Greek world.

- **460–377 BCE: Hippocrates**, known as the "Father of Medicine," is born on Kos. His work establishes the island as a center of medical knowledge. The **Asclepeion**, a sanctuary and healing center, attracts patients from across the Mediterranean and remains a cornerstone of medicine for centuries.

- **411 BCE**: During the **Peloponnesian War**, Kos faces heavy attacks from Sparta, particularly under Admiral **Astyochus**. Many residents flee, marking a temporary decline in the island's political and economic status.

- **334 BCE**: Kos allies with **Alexander the Great**, becoming a key military base for his eastern campaigns. In **332 BCE**, Alexander's admiral, **Amphoterus**, conquers the island, ushering in Macedonian influence.

- **323 BCE**: After Alexander's death, Kos becomes part of the **Ptolemaic Kingdom of Egypt**, entering a golden age of cultural flourishing in art and science.

- **205 BCE**: Kos forms a political and economic union with neighboring islands **Kalymnos** and **Nisyros**, further solidifying its regional power under Roman influence.

- **102 BCE**: **Cleopatra's visit** to Kos ends in tragedy as **Mithridates VI of Pontus** raids the island, seizing Cleopatra's treasures during his conflict with the Romans.

- **30 BCE**: A massive earthquake devastates Kos. Roman authorities initiate extensive reconstruction efforts, gradually restoring the island's prominence.

- **325 CE**: Kos becomes part of the **Byzantine Empire** under **Constantine the Great**. Christianity is declared the official religion, leading to the construction of churches and religious structures.

- **554 CE**: A catastrophic earthquake destroys much of Kos' infrastructure. Despite the devastation, the island is rebuilt under Byzantine rule.

- **1204**: Following the **Fourth Crusade**, Kos becomes part of **Venetian rule**, transforming into a princely state and experiencing cultural shifts as Venice consolidates its power in the region.

• **1457**: **18,000 Ottoman soldiers** invade and capture Kos, marking the beginning of centuries of **Ottoman rule**. The island enters a period of instability as part of the Ottoman Empire.

• **1912**: **Italian forces** land on Kos, ending Ottoman rule. The Italians initiate modernization projects, including infrastructure development, marking a new era for the island.

• **1934**: A devastating earthquake destroys much of Kos. Italian architects lead the reconstruction, leaving a legacy visible in the island's modern cityscape.

• **1945**: **British forces** liberate Kos from German occupation after World War II. The island remains under British administration temporarily while its future is decided.

• **1948**: Kos is finally united with **Greece** as part of the **Dodecanese islands**. This long-awaited reunion is a triumph for its people, who now fully integrate into the Greek nation.

• **1981**: As part of Greece, Kos joins the **European Union**, ushering in new economic and cultural opportunities. The island benefits from investments and becomes a thriving tourist destination.

Kos Town

STEP INTO THE HEART of Kos Town, where history and modern lifestyle merge in a city pulsing with energy and charm. Home to nearly **13,000 residents**, Kos Town is more than just a city—it is a tale of resurrection and timeless beauty.

Imagine a city rising from the ashes like a phoenix. In **1934**, after **80% of the town was reduced to ruins** by an earthquake, Italian architects brought their expertise to create a sparkling gem by the Aegean Sea. Today, Kos Town stands proud as a symbol of resilience and strength.

Whitewashed houses nestle side by side, surrounded by vibrant flowers and lush greenery, painting the city with a natural palette of beauty. Each street corner offers a visual delight, a symphony of contrasts harmonized into a unique aesthetic.

Explore the town's charm by **bicycle**, pedaling along the majestic **palm avenue** that embraces the fortress. Here, the past meets the present, and each turn reveals a new chapter of the city's rich history.

Pause at **Hippocrates' Tree**, a living monument that has stood as a witness to centuries. Dive into the city's soul through numerous **ancient excavations**, bringing the past vividly to life. Kos Town is an **architectural treasure**, shaped by the many cultures that have left their mark on its streets and squares.

Beaches

LET ME TAKE YOU ON a sun-soaked adventure to Kos' incredible beaches, where every stretch of sand feels like it's been tailor-made for your perfect day in paradise. Pack your sunscreen, because we're diving into some of the most beautiful seaside escapes the island has to offer!

Lambi Beach

Our first stop is Lambi Beach, right at the edge of Kos Town. This golden stretch of sand welcomes you with open arms and enough amenities to keep you in blissful relaxation. Getting here is a breeze—walk, bike, or hop on a bus. Whether you're soaking up the sun or simply letting the Aegean's waves wash your cares away, Lambi Beach is where time slows to a delicious crawl.

Agios Fokas Beach

Ready for something a little dramatic? Agios Fokas, just six kilometers south of Kos Town, greets us with black sands and pebbles glistening like stars. It's a peaceful retreat from the town's buzz, perfect for those lazy, wave-watching afternoons. Bonus: The trip here, whether by car, scooter, or bus, is as serene as the beach itself.

Tigaki Beach

Ah, Tigaki—the showstopper of Kos' coastline. Picture endless soft, white sands and a gentle sea breeze that whispers, "Stay a little longer." Whether you're lounging under the sun or letting the occasional waves tickle your toes, Tigaki blends tranquility with just the right amount of energy.

Paradise Beach

The name says it all. Paradise Beach, perched at the far end of Kefalos Bay, is the life of the beach party during summer. Sunbeds? Check. Parasols? Check. Water sports? Oh, absolutely. Whether you're chasing thrills or looking to chill, this beach has your back.

Camel Beach

Tucked snugly along the Kefalos coast, Camel Beach is a quieter gem. Its crystal-clear waters and a quirky camel-shaped rock formation make it the ideal spot for those Instagram-worthy sunset photos. It's low-key magic, pure and simple.

Cavo Paradiso

Feeling adventurous? Let's journey to Cavo Paradiso, a secluded haven at Kos' southern tip. The drive is a mini-adventure through rugged beauty, but trust me, the turquoise waters and unspoiled tranquility waiting at the end are worth it. Grab a drink at the tiny beach bar and let nature's masterpiece do the rest.

Kochilari Beach

Adrenaline junkies, this one's for you! Kochilari Beach, near Kefalos, is a mecca for kitesurfers. With steady winds and a dedicated kitesurfing station, it's the perfect playground. Not into surfing? No worries—there's plenty of quiet sand for a laid-back day by the waves.

Kamari Beach

Pebble-covered and peaceful, Kamari Beach offers a front-row seat to the charming Kastri Islet, complete with a tiny chapel. It's a serene spot for reflection—or just a cozy nap with the sound of waves lulling you into bliss.

Agios Theologos Beach

Let's head southwest to Agios Theologos, where rugged cliffs and hidden coves create a dramatic coastline perfect for exploration. Named after Saint John the Theologian, this beach feels like a world apart—a timeless retreat for the soul.

Kata Beach

Nearby, Kata Beach tempts us with turquoise waters, soft sands, and the intriguing sight of a shipwreck. It's peaceful, picturesque, and practically begs you to bring a picnic.

Kardamena Beach

Looking for family-friendly vibes? Kardamena Beach is your spot. Stretching for six kilometers, it's a sandy escape with clear waters and plenty of room to roam. The stunning Dikaios Mountains provide a postcard-perfect backdrop.

Mastichari Beach

A hop and a skip from Kos Town, Mastichari Beach offers golden sands, a charming harbor, and activities galore—think volleyball, windsurfing, and even a dreamy sunset to cap off your day.

Lakkos Beach

Finally, let's end on a peaceful note at Lakkos Beach. Nestled near Mastichari, this hidden treasure offers soft sands, crystal-clear waters, and a welcome break from the busier beaches. Perfect for quiet reflection or a refreshing swim.

Sights of Kos

———

KOS, THE ENCHANTING pearl of the Aegean Sea, feels like a living museum—a treasure chest of historical wonders that bring the past vividly to life. Every corner of this island invites you to step into another time, each site revealing layers of its rich history. As we journey through the zones of ancient Kos Town, you'll see the stories unfold with every step.

The Central Zone

———

WE START IN THE CENTRAL Zone, where history greets us at every turn. Picture this: as we wander through a maze of ancient ruins, the stones beneath our feet begin to whisper tales from the Mycenaean era through to early Christianity.

Look down—can you see the mosaics? These aren't just floor decorations; they're intricate stories woven in stone. One depicts **Asclepius**, the god of healing, while another honors **Hippocrates**, the man who redefined medicine. The artistry is astounding, and it feels as though these long-gone figures are guiding us through their world. These masterpieces now rest in the local museum, preserved as snapshots of a time when Kos was a hub of learning and innovation.

Rounding a corner, we stumble upon a **3rd-century CE pool** nestled in a serene courtyard. Water once flowed gently here, reflecting the sunlit mosaics that shimmer like a kaleidoscope of history. Close your eyes and imagine the sound of voices echoing off the walls—residents gathered here, sharing stories as water trickled softly nearby.

The Harbor Zone

NEXT, WE MOVE TOWARD the **Harbor Zone**, where the salty tang of the sea mixes with the echoes of an ancient world. Ahead of us loom the **4th-century BCE city walls**, their towering heights a testament to the fortitude and pride of Kos' past rulers. They seem to whisper of battles fought and won, their presence still commanding respect centuries later.

Just steps away, the **Sanctuary of Heracles** beckons. Here, under the warm glow of the sun, mosaics bring the tale of Orpheus to life. His mythical lyre serenades us, with scenes of wildlife surrounding him as if captured mid-song. The harmony of this place feels almost tangible, a moment of myth frozen in stone.

Venturing deeper, the **Agora** opens up before us. Can you picture the bustling marketplace it once was? Merchants shouting their wares, coins exchanging hands, and the hum of conversations filling the air. The columns that remain stand as stoic reminders of this lively scene, urging us to imagine the thriving heart of Kos in its prime.

As we follow the cobbled paths further, we arrive at the **Temple of Aphrodite**, a sanctuary dedicated to the goddess of love. Standing here, it's impossible not to feel a sense of awe. The devotion that must have radiated from this space lingers still, woven into the stones and carried by the gentle breeze off the sea.

Kos doesn't just tell its history—it lets you live it, step by step, zone by zone, as if the island itself is alive and eager to share its secrets. Ready to keep exploring? Let's move on to the Western Zone.

The Western Zone

STEP WITH ME INTO THE *Western Zone* of Kos, where the echoes of ancient life still resonate among the ruins. As we enter, the sight of the **gymnasium, Xysto**, greets us. Can you see it? Imagine its once-majestic colonnade stretching toward the sky. Today, only seventeen of the original 81 columns remain, standing tall like sentinels of the past, whispering stories of athletes who trained and competed here centuries ago.

Just a little further, the remnants of **ancient Christian basilicas** emerge, their foundations layered atop Roman baths. It's as if the structures themselves are bridging time, each stone holding secrets of the generations that walked these paths.

And then, there it is—the **Nymphaion**, a stunning 3rd-century public bath and toilet complex. Picture it alive with the sounds of splashing water and the hum of voices. The ancient Romans made even their baths places of grandeur, and here, you can feel the pulse of their daily lives.

But nothing prepares us for the **mosaic of The Abduction of Europa**. Look closer. It's breathtaking, isn't it? The scene unfolds dramatically: Zeus, transformed into a bull, surges through the waves with Europa on his back, her expression caught between fear and wonder. Overhead, Eros holds a burning torch, illuminating the narrative in a cascade of color and artistry.

Further along, we come to the **Odeion**, a cultural gem that still hosts performances today. Sitting on the ancient stone seats, you can almost hear the applause from 3rd-century audiences. Rediscovered in the 1930s by Italian archaeologist Luciano Laurenzi, this venue bridges past and present with every concert and play that graces its stage.

Finally, we arrive at **Casa Romana**, a time capsule of Roman elegance. The house feels alive, its three grand atriums welcoming us with intricate frescoes, mosaics, and marble floors. Can you imagine the life here? The sound of laughter in the banquet halls, the splash of water in the fountains? The mosaics are particularly captivating—mermaids that seem to shimmer, lions locked in fierce combat, and mythological figures that bring ancient stories vividly to life.

Casa Romana is a masterpiece of restoration and a must-see for anyone craving a connection to the vibrant, complex history of Kos.

The Eastern Zone

———

NOW, LET'S WANDER INTO the *Eastern Zone*, a space where even the stones feel heavy with history. Many of the original mosaics that once adorned this area now rest in the museum on Rhodes, but their legacy remains palpable. Among these treasures was the **Poseidon and Polyvotis mosaic**, a depiction of the sea god battling the giant Polyvotis. Though the original is gone, you can almost imagine the swirling waves and clashing titans right here where it was discovered.

The **fortress walls**, however, still stand in their full medieval glory. Within them lie the fragments of a time gone by—statues peeking out from history's veil, ancient cannons standing silently, and the remains of **Byzantine churches** and **4th-century CE houses**, all waiting for us to uncover their secrets.

The fortress itself is a marvel. Built during the Middle Ages, its **city walls**, constructed between 1390 and 1396, stretch imposingly across the landscape. Standing here, you can almost see the defenders preparing for battle, hear the clash of swords, and feel the resolve of a people safeguarding their home.

Each step we take through the *Eastern Zone* brings us closer to the heart of Kos' heritage. These ruins, these stones—they're more than relics; they're storytellers, inviting us to walk through their world and become part of the ever-unfolding narrative of this incredible island.

The Fortress of Kos Town

———

STEP THROUGH THE **Venetian arches** of Kos Town's Fortress, and you're immediately transported to another world. These grand arches, a striking reminder of the Venetian era's artistry, beckon you into a realm where medieval ingenuity meets ancient majesty. Picture this: a sprawling castle, meticulously constructed by the **Knights of St. John**, its walls imbued with the soul of the past, built from stones salvaged from ancient sanctuaries and temples. This blend of antiquity and medieval splendor is palpable in every crevice of the fortress.

As we wander inside, the fortress reveals itself like a treasure chest. **Statues stand silently**, their features worn by time but still commanding respect. Hidden **archaeological gems** peek out from corners, as though daring you to uncover their secrets. Each stone carries the weight of untold stories, and every turn feels like stepping further into a history book brought to life.

And then, we climb. Reaching the top of the fortress is a reward in itself. From here, the island unfolds beneath us, a breathtaking tableau of the **harbor's shimmering waters** and the lively **promenade**, where the old and new meet in perfect harmony. The view isn't just stunning—it's humbling, a reminder of the fortress's watchful role across centuries.

The Knights' City Walls

AS WE TRACE THE **Knights' City Walls**, it's hard not to marvel at their sheer presence. Built between 1391 and 1396, these walls weren't just a defense—they were a statement. They rise with a quiet authority, seamlessly interwoven with fragments of the **ancient city walls**, standing as a testament to Kos's resilience and ingenuity.

Walking along the path from **Akti Miaouli to Akti Kountouriotou**, you can almost hear the whispers of history carried by the wind. Over **Eleftherias Square** and down **Hippocrates Boulevard**, a moat once circled these defenses, adding to the city's impenetrable aura.

At the **eastern bastion**, your eyes catch the **coats of arms** of **Grand Master Heredia** and **Governor di Lango Fr. Hesso di Schwegelholz**, etched proudly into the walls. These symbols speak of the Knights' enduring legacy. To the northwest, a **round tower** stands tall, a silent sentinel that has seen centuries pass.

The journey leads us to the **Foros Gate**, a commanding entrance that opens onto a small square. Here, the **legendary Hippocrates Plane Tree** rises, a living link to the island's rich history and the great healer's enduring wisdom. Nearby, a **stone bridge** stretches across, connecting the city walls to the fortress itself, guiding us back to its sacred entrance.

Each step along these walls is a step through time, where every stone, every gate, and every view pulls you deeper into the narrative of Kos—an island that has defended its heart while embracing its history with pride.

The Loggia Mosque

LET ME TAKE YOU TO a corner of Kos where the island's **Ottoman heritage** quietly whispers its stories. The **Loggia Mosque**, built in **1786** by Turkish naval admiral **Yasa Irli Hasan**, stands with an air of timeless dignity near the entrance to the fortress. Its elegant design and enduring presence make it a poignant reminder of Kos's layered history.

As we stroll through the area, more architectural echoes of the **Ottoman era** come into view. The **Defendar Mosque**, nestled close to the bustling marketplace, still holds its ground as a silent observer of centuries gone by. And just down the road, at the corner of **Hippocrates and Mitropoleos Streets**, stands **Hadzi Pasha's Mausoleum**—a serene and intricate structure that feels like a portal to another time. Together, these monuments remain as **architectural jewels**, their beauty quietly but powerfully showcasing a bygone era's craftsmanship and legacy.

The Museum in Kos Town

———

AS WE STEP INTO THE **Museum in Kos Town**, it feels like walking into a **time capsule**, where every exhibit is a story waiting to unfold. Perched on **Eleftherias Square**, the museum is a vision of understated elegance—a perfect blend of historical charm and modern simplicity. Its design doesn't scream for attention; instead, it draws you in with a quiet promise of discovery.

The **foyer** sets the tone—a gateway into a world of wonders. Here, beneath the museum's minimalist architecture lies a rich **treasure trove of history**, meticulously preserved and beautifully displayed. Each artifact is a window to the past, from sacrificial altars in various shapes to **divine busts** like **Demeter** and **Agrippina the Younger**, standing tall with an almost regal presence, as though guarding their stories from the 1st century CE.

Moving deeper, your eyes are caught by **reliefs of animals**—horses galloping in frozen motion, lions prowling with an untamed spirit. And then comes the showstopper: a **mosaic** depicting **Asclepius's arrival on Kos**, where he is greeted by none other than **Hippocrates** and a local resident. The artistry, rich in color and detail, feels alive, pulling you into a scene from the **2nd or 3rd century CE**.

The museum doesn't stop there. Around the next corner are **statues from the 2nd century: Dionysus**, exuding an air of revelry, flanked by a mischievous **satyr** and the enigmatic **Pan**. Then there's **Artemis**, forever poised with her loyal hound by her side, embodying grace and determination.

Every corner of the museum offers a **new surprise**, a fresh glimpse into the island's ancient soul. It's not just a visit; it's a mesmerizing journey through the art, culture, and history that have shaped Kos.

Antimachia Fortress

———

AS WE ASCEND THE PLATEAU at the heart of Kos, **Antimachia Fortress** comes into view—a sprawling stronghold steeped in history and grandeur. Perched high above the island, it feels as though the fortress is keeping watch, a sentinel of the past. Built by the **Knights of St. John** between **1322 and 1346**, its imposing walls stretch an impressive **970 meters**, enclosing **26,250 square meters** of storied ground.

The **northwest gate** welcomes us into a labyrinth of pathways, each turn revealing echoes of medieval life. The sturdy stone walls speak of strategic brilliance, while remnants of fortifications and ancient cisterns whisper tales of resilience and ingenuity. The fortress isn't just an architectural marvel—it's a time machine, inviting us to walk in the footsteps of the knights who once defended its walls.

The Sanctuary of Asclepius

———

LET'S STEP INTO AN ancient world where medicine and divinity converged—a place where wisdom and healing flourished in perfect harmony. The **Sanctuary of Asclepius**, perched serenely atop a hill **100 meters above sea level**, invites us into its tranquil embrace. Surrounded by lush forests and springs that once bubbled with mineral-rich waters, it's easy to imagine the sanctuary as a haven for those seeking solace and restoration.

Asclepius, the god of medicine, carries a story as intricate as the sanctuary itself. Born of Apollo and the Thessalian princess Coronis, his tale is one of betrayal, divine wrath, and ultimate redemption. Raised by the wise centaur **Chiron** in the verdant woodlands of **Pelion**, Asclepius mastered the art of healing, earning reverence as both a mortal savior and a divine figure.

This sanctuary, known as an **Asclepieion**, is one of nearly **300 such sites** across ancient Greece. But the **Asclepieion of Kos** was special—a jewel among them. According to **Pausanias**, the sacred grove surrounding the temple was so hallowed that no one could be born or die there, preserving its purity and sanctity.

As we approach the site, a **cypress-lined pathway** welcomes us, leading to terraces that climb gracefully into the hillside:

- **The lower terrace**, with its serene colonnades and fountains, feels like a gentle introduction, inviting us to pause and reflect.

- **The middle terrace**, home to the ruins of a **Doric temple dedicated to Asclepius**, reveals fragments of a sacred space where prayers for healing once echoed.

44

- **The upper terrace** crowns the sanctuary with its grand temple, built in the **2nd century BCE**. Here, statues of **Asclepius** and **Hygieia** stand as timeless sentinels of a world where divine healing met the transformative power of the Hippocratic tradition.

Rediscovered in **1899** by German archaeologist **Herzog**, with the unwavering belief of local resident **Jakovos Zaraftis**, the sanctuary's ancient stones were brought back to light.

Exploring the **Asclepieion of Kos** feels like stepping into a sacred story—one where medicine, faith, and the pursuit of wellness were woven together to leave a legacy that inspires even today.

Exploring the Villages of Kos

GRAB YOUR HAT AND SUNGLASSES—WE'RE setting off on an adventure through the **picturesque villages of Kos**, where nature greets us with open arms and history whispers from every corner. These villages are like pearls waiting to be strung into a necklace of unforgettable memories. Let's dive in together, shall we?

Antimachia and Mastichari - Ancient Roots and Coastal Charm

First stop, **Antimachia**, a village so old it could have its own chapter in Greek mythology. Nestled on a lush plateau near the airport, this place boasts a history stretching back over **3,000 years**. Legend has it, Antimachia was named after **Antimahos**, son of Heracles—talk about having big sandals to fill! The locals, wise as ever, moved inland to dodge pirates and other unsavory characters who liked to pop by uninvited.

But it wasn't all smooth sailing. On **April 23, 1926**, Antimachia became the epicenter of an earthquake that rattled Kos with a 5.4 on the Richter scale. Houses crumbled, and two lives were tragically lost. Some families decided to swap the plateau for the seaside, settling in what's now known as **Mastichari**, a village planned out by the Italians in 1930. Picture neat streets laid out like a game of tic-tac-toe, surrounded by mastic trees and the endless blue of the Aegean.

Today, Mastichari offers golden sands and a history as deep as its waters. Did you know it once hosted a German-built pier during WWII? That's right—the village's past involves both war-time logistics and watermelons (yes, watermelons), which were shipped to Kalymnos from Mastichari's shores. Who knew fruit could have such a rich history?

Asfendiou and Zia - Lush Greens and Endless Views

Next, let's head up to **Asfendiou**, perched at the base of **Mount Dikaios** like a cat curled up for an afternoon nap. Here lies **Zia**, a village so pretty it could make postcards jealous. Imagine strolling through streets lined with vibrant flowers, listening to trickling springs, and breathing in the scent of freshly baked bread wafting from nearby tavernas. Sounds like a dream, right?

Zia isn't just about looks—it's got heart, too. The locals, warm and welcoming, are always ready with a story (or a bottle of ouzo, depending on the time of day). Make your way to **Kefalovrissi**, a lookout point that offers panoramic views so stunning they might leave you questioning why you ever considered going anywhere else. From here, you can see the sea stretching endlessly, with islands sprinkled across the horizon like a chef's final garnish.

Assomatos and Evangelistria - Where Stone Meets Spirit

Hold onto your sandals as we venture into **Assomatos**, a village that feels like stepping back in time. The **Assomatos Church** is the centerpiece here, not just spiritually but economically—it once handed out loans to farmers and helped build schools. Talk about divine intervention!

The stone houses here have stories etched into every corner, their bamboo or timber roofs blending harmoniously with the surrounding mountains. It's a place where nature and humanity have danced together for centuries, and every step feels like you're discovering a hidden rhythm.

Nearby, **Evangelistria** beckons with its beautifully restored houses and a history steeped in resilience. A stroll through its cobbled paths might lead you to abandoned olive presses or the neighboring **Pera Geitonia**, where even the air feels heavy with the past.

Zipari and Pyli - Secrets Beneath the Surface

Next up, **Zipari**, a village that's keeping it cool in the Kos lowlands. Modern and vibrant, it's the kind of place where you could grab a frappé and stumble upon ancient ruins without even trying. The **Analipsis Church** stands tall here, alongside the remnants of early Christian basilicas.

A short drive later, and we're in **Pyli**, a place where legends and landscapes collide. It's not every day you find a **3rd-century royal tomb** next to lush springs and thriving farmland. And did I mention the **Eleusinian temple ruins** uncovered by an Italian archaeologist in the 1920s? Pyli has layers, and we're peeling them back together, one ancient whisper at a time.

Kefalos - Coastal Magic and Windswept Adventures

Ready for some beach vibes? Let's head to **Kefalos**, where fishermen hum sea shanties and the sand is so soft it feels like walking on powdered sugar. The **Agios Stefanos Basilica**, perched by the water, adds a touch of history to your seaside escape. And if you're feeling adventurous, try your hand at windsurfing or parasailing—the sea here is as inviting as a Greek grandmother with a platter of spanakopita.

Don't miss **Kastri Islet**, home to the humble **Agios Antonios Church**, or the volcanic **Paradissos Beach**, where underwater bubbles rise like little secrets escaping the earth's core. Whether you're soaking up the sun or exploring ancient ruins, Kefalos is the kind of place that makes you forget your flight home.

Zia - A Sunset Worth the Climb

Our last stop is **Zia**, nestled high on **Mount Dikaios** like a crown jewel. This village is famous for its **sunsets**, which paint the sky in hues so spectacular, you might want to frame them. Hike up to the **Christos Church** for views that stretch all the way to Turkey and beyond.

After working up an appetite, settle into a taverna where the food is as rich as the stories you've just uncovered. Start with a sip of ouzo, nibble on some **mezedakia**, and finish with a plate of **galaktoboureko** that might just convince you to move here permanently.

The Natural Wonders of Kos

PACK YOUR SENSE OF adventure—we're heading off to discover Kos' most stunning natural landscapes together. From dramatic cliffs to hidden caves, we'll tackle the rugged beauty of the island, step by step, trail by trail. Ready? Let's go!

Cape Krikelos - Where the Wild Meets the Spectacular

Our journey begins at **Cape Krikelos**, the wild southwestern tip of Kos. The terrain here feels raw and untamed, with sparse Mediterranean greenery stretching out to meet the blue horizon. It's rugged, it's beautiful, and it's calling to us. We'll make our way through the **pines near Aghios Mammas**, a touch of unexpected lushness that breaks up the rocky scenery.

The **views from Cape Krikelos** are nothing short of breathtaking—trust me, it's worth every bead of sweat. To get there, we'll follow the road toward Aghios Mammas before venturing off the beaten path. Literally. There are no proper trails here, just **narrow goat tracks** that we'll navigate carefully.

We'll stick to the **right-hand side** as we approach the cape to avoid the trickiest parts of the terrain. On the way back toward **Cavo Paradiso**, we'll find a gentler route. Keep right, steer clear of the cliff's edge, and enjoy the moment. Sure, the rocks can be slippery, but don't worry—I've got you. Look at these **rock formations**, shaped by centuries of wind and waves. Don't they look like they belong in a mythical tale?

Cape Routhianos - The Path Less Traveled

From here, we're heading to **Cape Routhianos**, tucked just below the **Aspri Petra Cave**. To get there, we'll follow a dusty trail that winds its way through the hills. The path isn't perfect—winter rains sometimes carve their marks—but it's nothing we can't handle.

And oh, the reward waiting for us! When we arrive, we'll stand together at the edge of this natural wonder, soaking in views that make the effort so, so worth it.

The Caves of Kefalos - Secrets Beneath the Surface

Now, let's delve underground, shall we? Beneath the charming village of Kefalos lies a hidden world: **the caves**. Just **100 meters from the iconic windmill**, these ancient formations feel like nature's own treasure chest.

As we step inside, you'll notice the porous rock, worn away over centuries into intricate shapes. These caves aren't just pretty—they've got stories to tell. They've been shelters for goats, storage rooms, and perhaps even secret hideaways. Look around—can you imagine the lives that have passed through here?

Exploring these caves is like uncovering a forgotten chapter of Kos' history. Together, we'll let our imaginations run wild as we navigate their cool, shadowy depths.

The Kezi Mountains - Where Earth Meets Sky

Our final stop takes us to the majestic **Kezi Mountains**, where every step offers a fresh perspective. As we climb the winding paths, let's pause to take it all in: **soaring cliffs**, **towering treetops**, and the sea glinting like liquid sapphire in the distance.

These trails have a way of making you feel small in the best possible way. The **rock formations** seem almost sculpted by an artist, and the air carries a freshness that's impossible to describe. Let's take our time here—there's no rush. With every turn, nature reveals another masterpiece, and I want you to savor every single one.

Mount Thymianos - Where History Meets Nature

We'll start our journey at **Mount Thymianos**, rising 450 meters above sea level in the southwestern part of Kefalos. As we climb, the air fills with the unmistakable aroma of wild thyme, the herb that gave this mountain its name. But our destination isn't just about fragrant foliage—it's about the stunning **Aghios Ioannis Thymianos Church**, also known as **Krikelos**, perched gracefully on the mountain's western slope.

The history here is palpable. During **World War II**, the Italians built four lighthouses to guide planes to a nearby airfield. Imagine this serene mountaintop bustling with activity as seven machine-gun posts guarded the bright beacons, each mounted on 8-meter-high towers. In **September 1944**, German forces stormed the site, destroying the lighthouses, power generators, and every building in sight. Today, among the ruins, we'll see remnants of the control room, gun emplacements, and even shrapnel scars—silent witnesses to a night of chaos.

Plaka - A Forest Oasis with Feathers and Charm

Next, we'll head toward **Plaka**, just a short detour from the main road to Kefalos. As we leave the bustling roundabout by the airport, the scenery shifts dramatically. Soon, a side road beckons us into a green paradise—a **pine forest** that spills down into the shimmering blue of the Aegean Sea.

Walking into Plaka feels like stepping into a fairytale. The air is cooler, fresher, and carries the soft scent of pine and wildflowers. Beneath the trees, **peacocks strut their stuff**, their vibrant plumage glinting like living jewels. Benches along the trails invite us to pause, breathe, and soak in the serenity.

Plaka's charm goes beyond nature. During the Italian occupation, this area was developed around a natural spring, and the tradition of roasting lamb and goat over open pits for Easter still lingers. The road continues toward Antimachia and Kefalos, but for now, let's sit under the whispering trees and enjoy the moment.

Plakeri - Nature's Stone Cathedral

Feeling adventurous? Let's tackle **Plakeri**, a stunning site near the summit of **Mount Dikaios**, Kos' highest point. Here, nature shows off with massive stone slabs that jut dramatically into the sky, like a giant's playground.

The climb isn't easy—expect narrow trails and a few challenges along the way—but every step is rewarded with **panoramic views** that stretch across the island. From these vantage points, the surrounding landscape unfolds like a living map, with the sea shimmering in the distance and rugged terrain rolling beneath us.

As we navigate the trails, the massive rocks take on intricate, otherworldly shapes. It's as if nature itself has sculpted a masterpiece just for us. And when we reach the top, where **Christos Church** stands proudly, the sense of achievement is unmatched.

Christos Church and the Legacy of Mount Dikaios

At the peak of **Mount Dikaios**, or **Oromedon**, we find **Christos Church**, dedicated to the Transfiguration of Christ. Built on the ruins of a Byzantine-era church, this sacred site has stood since the 13th century, its stones whispering tales of faith and resilience.

The trail to the summit begins in **Monagri** and winds through tranquil forests. The journey is demanding, especially in the summer heat, but shaded spots along the way offer welcome relief. As we ascend, the sounds of the forest—chirping birds, rustling leaves, the occasional goat bleating—provide a soothing soundtrack.

When we finally reach the church, we're greeted with a breathtaking view of **Psilo Vouno**, the island's highest point, and the surrounding islands shimmering on the horizon. The air feels lighter here, the world quieter. This is more than a hike; it's a spiritual connection to the island itself.

Good to Know

———

THE EMBASSY AND FOREIGN Affairs

Let's start with the boring-but-necessary stuff: **embassies and travel safety**. If you need assistance, the **Norwegian Embassy in Athens** is your go-to. They're located at Good to Know: A Practical and Flavorful Guide to Kos

The Embassy and Foreign Affairs

If you find yourself in need of assistance while on Kos, the **British Embassy in Athens** is your best point of contact. Here's all the information you need:

- **Address:** 1 Ploutarchou Street, 106 75 Athens

- **Phone:** +30 210 7272 600

- **Email:** information.athens@fcdo.gov.uk

Please note that visits must be arranged in advance. You can reach them for phone inquiries from **Monday to Friday, 8:00 AM to 3:00 PM.**

For **consular assistance**, you can email the consular team at **consular.athens@fcdo.gov.uk**. In case of emergencies outside regular office hours, the **British Foreign Service** offers 24/7 support through their online inquiry system.

For up-to-date travel advice and safety tips, visit the embassy's official website[1]. And don't forget to register your travel plans through the **UK**

———

1. https://www.gov.uk/world/organisations/british-embassy-athens

Foreign, Commonwealth & Development Office's travel app, so you're prepared for any unexpected situations.

Remember, the embassy is closed on British and Greek public holidays, so plan ahead for any required services!

Tipping Etiquette

Now for something lighter: **tipping**. While tips are often included in bills at restaurants or in taxis, it's customary to leave an extra **5–10%** for stellar service. Hotel staff and other service workers will also appreciate a small token of your gratitude, whether it's a coin or two or a big smile to go with it.

Public Holidays on Kos and in Greece

Here's a pro tip: don't plan your shopping spree on a Greek holiday—shops and banks will likely be closed. Here's the cheat sheet:

- **January 1:** New Year's Day

- **January 6:** Epiphany

- **March 25:** Independence Day (celebrating the start of the 1821 revolution—fireworks likely included!)

- **Easter:** Greece's most important holiday, following the Julian calendar (pro tip: it often falls after Western Easter).

- **May 1:** May Day ("Protomagia"), a day for flower-picking, wreath-making, and general merriment.

- **August 15:** The Dormition of the Virgin Mary

- **October 28:** Oxi Day ("No Day"), commemorating Greece's defiant refusal to Mussolini in 1940.

• **December 25–26:** Christmas and Boxing Day

Food and Drink - A Feast for Your Taste Buds

Ah, now we're in my favorite territory: food! Whether you're a fan of hearty meals, fresh seafood, or sweet treats, **Kos' culinary scene** will spoil you. Here's a menu of local favorites we're about to indulge in:

- **Souvlaki:** Grilled meat on skewers—simple, smoky, and delicious.

- **Moussaka:** Layers of eggplant, potato, minced meat, and creamy béchamel—comfort food at its finest.

- **Fasolada:** Greece's beloved bean soup, a bowl of warmth made with tomatoes, onions, and olive oil.

- **Kleftiko:** Lamb slow-cooked with herbs until it melts in your mouth.

- **Greek Salad:** Juicy tomatoes, crunchy cucumbers, feta, and olives drizzled in virgin olive oil.

- **Tzatziki:** That cool, garlicky yogurt dip you'll want to slather on everything.

- **Dolmades:** Grape leaves stuffed with seasoned rice, light and bursting with flavor.

- **Saganaki:** Fried cheese heaven—add a squeeze of lemon, and you're set.

- **Octopus:** Grilled to perfection and served seaside—nothing says "Greek island" like this.

- **Baklava:** Flaky pastry filled with nuts and honey—a sweet finish to any meal.

Local tavernas often serve these delights in relaxed settings where you can sip on a **Raki** or **Ouzo**.

- **Raki:** A potent grape spirit that packs a punch.

- **Ouzo:** An anise-flavored aperitif that turns cloudy with water—a theatrical treat for your taste buds.

Kos isn't just about eating; it's about **feasting**—on food, stories, and the scenery around you. Whether at a family-owned taverna or a seaside restaurant, you'll find that every bite tells a story of tradition and passion.

Athens. You can call them at **+30 210 72 46 173** or email them at **emb.athens@mfa.no**. Heads up, they like to keep things organized, so make sure to schedule your visit in advance. They're available for calls Monday through Friday, from **9:30 AM to 2:00 PM**.

For the extra-prepared travelers, download Norway's **"Reiseklar" app**. It offers up-to-date travel advice and lets you register your trip for emergencies—a little insurance against the unexpected.

Tipping Etiquette

Now for something lighter: **tipping**. While tips are often included in bills at restaurants or in taxis, it's customary to leave an extra **5–10%** for stellar service. Hotel staff and other service workers will also appreciate a small token of your gratitude, whether it's a coin or two or a big smile to go with it.

Public Holidays on Kos and in Greece

Here's a pro tip: don't plan your shopping spree on a Greek holiday—shops and banks will likely be closed. Here's the cheat sheet:

- **January 1:** New Year's Day

- **January 6:** Epiphany

- **March 25:** Independence Day (celebrating the start of the 1821 revolution—fireworks likely included!)

- **Easter:** Greece's most important holiday, following the Julian calendar (pro tip: it often falls after Western Easter).

- **May 1:** May Day ("Protomagia"), a day for flower-picking, wreath-making, and general merriment.

- **August 15:** The Dormition of the Virgin Mary

- **October 28:** Oxi Day ("No Day"), commemorating Greece's defiant refusal to Mussolini in 1940.

- **December 25–26:** Christmas and Boxing Day

Food and Drink - A Feast for Your Taste Buds

Ah, now we're in my favorite territory: food! Whether you're a fan of hearty meals, fresh seafood, or sweet treats, **Kos' culinary scene** will spoil you. Here's a menu of local favorites we're about to indulge in:

- **Souvlaki:** Grilled meat on skewers—simple, smoky, and delicious.

- **Moussaka:** Layers of eggplant, potato, minced meat, and creamy béchamel—comfort food at its finest.

- **Fasolada:** Greece's beloved bean soup, a bowl of warmth made with tomatoes, onions, and olive oil.

- **Kleftiko:** Lamb slow-cooked with herbs until it melts in your mouth.

- **Greek Salad:** Juicy tomatoes, crunchy cucumbers, feta, and olives drizzled in virgin olive oil.

- **Tzatziki:** That cool, garlicky yogurt dip you'll want to slather on everything.

- **Dolmades:** Grape leaves stuffed with seasoned rice, light and bursting with flavor.

- **Saganaki:** Fried cheese heaven—add a squeeze of lemon, and you're set.

- **Octopus:** Grilled to perfection and served seaside—nothing says "Greek island" like this.

- **Baklava:** Flaky pastry filled with nuts and honey—a sweet finish to any meal.

Local tavernas often serve these delights in relaxed settings where you can sip on a **Raki** or **Ouzo**.

- **Raki:** A potent grape spirit that packs a punch.

- **Ouzo:** An anise-flavored aperitif that turns cloudy with water—a theatrical treat for your taste buds.

Kos isn't just about eating; it's about **feasting**—on food, stories, and the scenery around you. Whether at a family-owned taverna or a seaside restaurant, you'll find that every bite tells a story of tradition and passion.

Local Wines - A Toast to the Heritage of Kos

EXPLORING THE LOCAL wines of Kos is like sipping history from a glass. Each wine tells a story of the island's unique climate, fertile soil, and proud vinicultural traditions. Let's swirl, sniff, and sip our way through Kos' most celebrated varietals:

White Wines: Fresh, Floral, and Fabulous

- **Assyrtiko:** A superstar of the Mediterranean climate, this white grape produces crisp, mineral-driven wines with vibrant acidity. Perfect with grilled fish and seafood, it's also used to craft sweet wines that are elegantly timeless.

- **Aidani:** Floral and fruity, Aidani adds depth and complexity to blends. Its gentle bouquet of aromas whispers tales of Kos' sunlit hillsides.

- **Athiri:** Light, refreshing, and delightfully citrusy, Athiri offers floral notes and a lively profile. It's an easy-drinking white for any occasion.

- **Malagousia:** Originally from mainland Greece, this aromatic grape has found a home on Kos. It delivers white wines bursting with citrus and floral elegance, making it a favorite among those seeking a vibrant sip.

Red Wines: Bold, Spicy, and Rich

- **Mavrotragano:** This powerful red grape is all about bold flavors of ripe red fruit and spices. Its structured tannins and richness make it ideal for fans of fuller-bodied reds.

- **Mandilaria:** Deep, robust, and intensely colored, Mandilaria is the choice for those who crave wines with body and complexity. Its dark berry notes make it unforgettable.

Traditional Styles

- **Nykteri:** Translating to "working all night," this traditional white wine style involves late-day grape harvesting and natural fermentation. The result? Full-bodied wines with layers of complexity and richness.

Discovering Kos' Wine Legacy

Each wine is a sip of Kos' vinicultural heritage, reflecting the island's diverse terroir and timeless techniques. Whether you prefer a crisp white or a bold red, these varietals are a testament to the islanders' passion for winemaking.

Vineyards to Visit

FOR A TRULY IMMERSIVE experience, take a trip to Kos' **boutique wineries**. Here, you can tour the vineyards, learn about traditional and modern winemaking practices, and, of course, enjoy tastings of these local treasures. Many wineries also offer breathtaking views of the countryside, making your visit both delicious and picturesque. Each vineyard offers a story worth savoring. Here are some must-visit wineries:

- **Hatzidakis Winery** (Antimachia): Known for its diverse range of wines, including refreshing whites, robust reds, and luscious dessert wines. Traditional production methods ensure an authentic taste of Kos' terroir.

- **Triantafyllopoulos Vineyards** (Asfendiou): Specializing in organic wines made from local grape varieties like Assyrtiko and Aidani. The breathtaking setting adds to this sustainable and authentic wine experience.

- **Tsalapatis Winery** (Pyli): A family-run vineyard offering a variety of wines in a charming and traditional environment. Perfect for wine lovers eager to dive into the local flavors.

- **Panteli Vineyards** (Lagoudi): Known for organic wines and spectacular views, this vineyard focuses on sustainable production using local grape varieties for a unique wine experience.

- **Kefalos Winery** (Kefalos): Famous for its warm hospitality and guided cellar tours, this vineyard gives visitors a deeper understanding of Kos' rich wine heritage.

It's a good idea to call ahead to confirm opening hours and book your visit. Exploring these vineyards is a delicious journey through the flavors of Kos' unique terroir.

Be Prepared - A Practical Guide to Your Trip

———

MOSQUITOES

Let's face it—these tiny pests can be a nuisance on Kos. Keep a trusty mosquito spray handy, and consider using an electric plug-in mosquito repellent in your room. For evenings on the balcony, mosquito candles create both ambiance and protection.

Emergency Numbers

While we hope you won't need them, here are the essential emergency numbers:

- **Ambulance:** 166

- **Fire Brigade:** 199

- **Police:** 100

Passports and Visas

UK citizens can travel visa-free to Greece for up to 90 days. Make sure your passport is valid for the entire duration of your stay. For families, ensure every child has their own passport.

Smoking Regulations

Kos takes smoking laws seriously. Smoking is prohibited in public transport, government buildings, and airports. However, many cafés, restaurants, and tavernas offer designated smoking areas, so you can still enjoy your puff in the summer breeze.

Safety

Kos is generally safe, with low crime rates. Still, exercise common sense—keep an eye on your belongings and stay aware of your surroundings.

Electricity

No need for adapters! Kos uses 220V power and the same plugs as the UK.

Health

Carry your European Health Insurance Card (EHIC) and get travel insurance for extra peace of mind. If you need medical assistance, keep all receipts for potential reimbursement.

Time Zone

Kos operates on Eastern European Time (EET, UTC+2) and Eastern European Summer Time (EEST, UTC+3) during daylight saving months. Meanwhile, England follows Greenwich Mean Time (GMT, UTC+0) and British Summer Time (BST, UTC+1) in summer. This means Kos is usually two hours ahead of England, but during summer, the gap shrinks to just one hour when both switch to daylight saving time.

Tourist Tax

Since January 2018, Greece has implemented a tourist tax:

- **2-star hotels:** €0.50 per night

- **3-star hotels:** €1.50 per night

- **4-star hotels:** €3.00 per night

- **5-star hotels:** €4.00 per night

Payable at your accommodation, usually at check-out. Most places prefer cash.

Water

Although tap water on Kos is safe to drink, it's chlorinated and may not taste great. Stick to bottled water for drinking, but tap water is fine for boiling, cooking, and making coffee or tea.

Currency

The currency in Kos is the euro (€). ATMs are plentiful, and most offer English instructions. Visa and Mastercard are widely accepted.

Kos awaits with its rich history, delicious wines, and practical ease. Here's to a wonderful, well-prepared adventure—**yammas!**

Safe Travels!

———

AND JUST LIKE THAT, we've reached the end of my Kos travel tale. I hope you've picked up a few helpful tips for your own adventure. Maybe you're already soaking up the sun on this magical island, in which case I hope my stories have added a sprinkle of inspiration to your trip. If your plans are still in the works, let me leave you with some advice to help you find your perfect slice of paradise.

Kos might not have the same wild, party-hard reputation it once did, but there's still a vibe for every type of traveler. If you're chasing nightlife and energy, **Kos Town** and **Kardamena** are buzzing with action. On the other hand, if peace and authenticity are more your style, the island's smaller towns and villages will be your haven.

Take **Tigaki**, for example—a charming little spot with a great mix of restaurants and bars, perfect for chilled-out evenings. Then there's **Marmari**, a smaller village with its own unique charm and a more low-key selection of amenities. Both places boast stunning, expansive sandy beaches where you can relax for days, with the waves gently lapping at your feet.

Whether you're here for the lively adventures or the quiet, authentic moments, I hope your days on Kos are filled with unforgettable experiences and treasured memories—just like this island has gifted me and my family over the years.

Bon voyage and happy exploring!